35 Wel Will Pay You to Write

By Writing Axis

"A great resource for writers who need regular work that pays well." — HBC Book Reviews

The rise of the gig economy has provided more opportunities than ever for writers to profit while working remotely. Whether you're looking to launch a writing career, supplement your income or increase your earning potential by writing for high-paying, big-name brands, this is the only resource you need.

Includes:

- 35 websites that provide regular work for writers
- Sites that pay up to $800 per article, $70 per hour and $1.75 per word
- In-depth overviews providing insight into each opportunity
- Links to the websites, so you can easily apply

Perfect for:

- Established freelancers who want to earn big by writing for large brands
- Full-time writers in search of regular remote work
- People looking to earn extra income, build a portfolio and establish a writing career
- People with writing skills who want to supplement their income with well-paying part-time work

Other books by Writing Axis:

Kindle Book Marketing:
A Brief Guide for How to Sell More Books

TABLE OF CONTENTS

List of 35 Paying Websites

#1

Skyword

Overview

Skyword brands itself as specializing in "The art and science of content marketing." What this really means is the company serves clients in search of agency-style content marketing.

From a writer's perspective, Skyword provides opportunities to earn money writing for some very big brands. Of course, Skyword takes a cut, but there's still some very good money left over afterword. At Skyword, writers can earn from $150 to $800 per article, especially if you can provide good ghostwriting and tech content.

Skyword has two ways of operating: They offer the full-service setup for clients where they plan a specific content strategy, set the writer's pay rate, and act as intermediary between the client and writer. Skyword also allows companies to search its writer pool and select writers. Whatever the case, there are big opportunities if you can earn a place in the Skyword writers pool.

FROM THE WEBSITE:

Skyword connects exceptional writers, graphic designers, videographers, photographers, and other creatives with top-tier brands looking to truly connect with their audiences through great storytelling.

An Elite Creative Community

Our contributor community is a big reason why our clients trust Skyword to craft their branded stories. We review every portfolio in detail to ensure that our community is comprised of the best of the best

Our platform handles assignments, scheduling, and payment, so you can concentrate on doing what you do best.

Top Brands, Elite Writers & Creatives

Join now for the opportunity to do the best work of your career for globally recognized brands. Skyword is growing, and our customers are constantly searching for freelancers who specialize in a number of specific areas.

Get the guidelines and details about Skyword at:

https://www.skyword.com/create-for-skyword/

#2

Writer Access

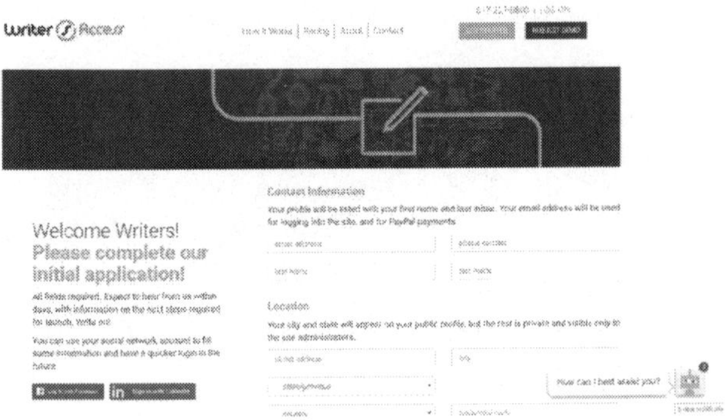

Overview

If you're looking for high pay, Writer Access isn't going to be your best option. A writer can only expect to make between $.014 and $.07 per word. What's more, you have to prove your worth by submitting consistent quality work before you will be allowed to claim higher-paying projects.

With that said, the platform does provide regular work which can keep you busy if you're looking to make some extra money or build up your portfolio. It also provides opportunities for for editors, translators, and content strategists. These jobs start at approximately $21 each near the bottom. If you work your way up, however, you can claim projects that pay up to $70 per hour.

Just like most writer's mills, Writer's Access has its drawbacks. It can be useful, however, if you need to get some experience, build up a lackluster portfolio or make ends meet while you look for a higher-paying opportunity.

FROM THE WEBSITE:

You have the amazing talent. We have amazing jobs(remote)!

Remote work is now the mainstream, offering benefits that make life better, and more fun. With all our freelance talent in the platform working remotely and global expansion now in the works, we decided to join the distributed workforce revolution in 2019 and beyond.

We're currently looking for remote part-time and full-time staff members that can provide exceptional solutions, personalized service and passionate delight to our customers, talent and fans.

Why choose us? Growth for all.
Keen values. Keener bonuses. Our strategic plan and core values drive our growth. Each employee single-handedly represents our brand, driven by individual, department and company goals-- all tied to generous bonuses.

The customer journey. Suprise and delight.

Our secret is enhancing the customer experience throughout their journey. We dream up fun new ways to WOW customers and talent, nearly every day.

Career advancement. Are you ready? Where do you want to go? We want to help you get there.

Our commitment to our team members includes helping you learn, grow and advance in amazing ways.

You will find Writer Access's guidelines and submission details at:

https://www.writeraccess.com/apply-writer/

#3

Horizon Edition Magazine

Overview

This in-flight trade magazine is distributed to flights for Horizon Air. Read by more than half a million travelers every month, it pays very good money for well-written relevant articles.

Since the magazine is 80 percent freelance written, the editors are constantly in search of quality material. Pay rates start at $100 for The Region section, a series of short (200 to 500 words) profiles and news articles from around the Pacific Northwest.

Rates for departments, which may include industry and corporate profiles, travel and community profiles, and regional-issue analyses start at $250; departments run about 1,600 words in length. The magazine also pays $450 for feature articles of up to 2,000 to 2,500 words.

FROM THE WEBSITE:

We look for writing with vivid images, anecdotes and a strong narrative flow. We are always looking for writers of national-magazine caliber, who can cover business and travel with style and insight. Horizon Edition Magazine is 80 percent freelance written.

The best way for writers to get started with us is to send clips of published work (photocopies are fine) and a well-written query, including a sample lead that represents the direction, tone and style proposed for the story. The query should demonstrate advance research and original thought on the part of the writer.

Rates begin at $100 for The Region section, a series of short (200 to 500 words) news articles and profiles from around the Pacific Northwest. Rates for departments, which may include corporate and industry profiles, regional-issue analysis, and travel and community profiles, start at $250; departments run about 1,600 words in length. Feature rates start at $450 for 2,000 to 2,500 words.

Assignments are formally acknowledged by written contract. Horizon Edition Magazine pays on publication, buying first-time printing rights with reprint rights and digital/archival rights. We pay a kill-fee of one-third the contracted assignment fee. Expenses, agreed to in advance, are paid on invoice. Expenses and rates vary in special circumstances.

Queries will not be accepted over the telephone or via e-mail. Features should be queried at least six months in advance. We respond if the story matches our needs. Be sure to include your telephone number and email address, but there is no need to include a self-addressed stamped envelope. Please do not send original manuscripts, artwork or slides, as we cannot be responsible for their receipt, or their return.

You will find Horizon Edition Magazine's guidelines and submission details at:

http://www.alaskaairlinesmagazine.com/horizonedition/guidelines/contributor/

#4

Great Escape Publishing

What's Going On

Overview

Focusing on the business and craft of paid travel, Great Escape Publishing will pay between $50 and $200 for quality articles.

Their audience mostly consists of people in search of opportunities to make a living while traveling. Think tour guides, photographers, cruise staff and travel writers. They will also pay $150 for brief interviews with professionals who work in the travel and hospitality industry.

Before submitting a piece, be sure to read their style guidelines. Great Escape Publishing also recommends that you look over their newsletter to get a better sense of what they're looking for.

Submissions should be sent as docx or doc files and should include your full name, address and telephone number. Limit your word count to approximately 300-600 words.

FROM THE WEBSITE:

Submissions should be sent as a .doc or .docx file, include your full name, address and telephone number, and be approximately 300-600 words for publication in The Right Way to Travel. We purchase all rights to the articles we publish and non-exclusive unlimited use rights to the images. Payment is upon publication. We retain the right to publish your article/photos in any of our affiliated publications as well as the World Wide Web.

We pay $150 for interviews, personal stories, and any articles we request for the website with specific income advice readers can print and follow to earn more income.

If requested by the employees of Great Escape Publishing, the author will verify all facts in the article and furnish the fact-checking material to Great Escape Publishing, including a list of sources and/or footnotes backing up each claim made, facts/research cited and sources included in the work.

You will find Great Escape Publishing's guidelines and submission details at:

https://www.greatescapepublishing.com/writers-guidelines/

#5

Transitions Abroad

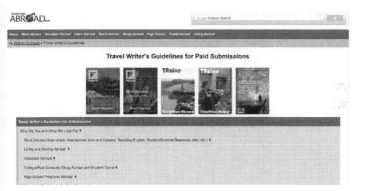

Overview

Transitions Abroad focuses on readers who travel either for leisure, work, education, retirement or as part of volunteering programs.

You can expect to earn approximately $150 for any accepted travel-themed article. The publication is especially interested in information-based pieces, along with articles written based on a writer's personal experience.

If you enjoy traveling or have a lot of travel experience, Transitions Abroad is a great potential outlet for your work. Be aware, however, that the publication has some pretty comprehensive writing guidelines. So, be sure to thoroughly read these over before you even think of submitting your piece.

FROM THE WEBSITE:

What We Look for in Editorial Style

Useful, practical information gained from first-hand experience and geared to readers who travel to immerse themselves abroad while respecting the culture and land of the people whose countries (homes) are being visited (while preferably spending money that benefits local economies directly).

Articles that inspire others to enjoy and explore off-the-beaten track travel respecting natives, their culture, and the land being visited. TransitionsAbroad.com is primarily a space for travelers and travel writers to share information with an emphasis on the practical yet inspirational, or what is currently called "transformational travel" and avoiding overtourism at locations that are saturated.

Content must be information-based. The editors are unable to check all sources, so current and accurate information is essential. Try to approach travel writing as an engaged journalist wishing to share important and exciting information with others. Be as concise as possible and do not hesitate to offer your own documented critical evaluations.

In-depth articles that explore a subject with authority. The web has matured over the years and there is much information on almost any subject under the sun. What differentiates an article on any subject over another is the authority with which you write and the depth of the knowledge you have gained from your experience.

Box outs should ideally include resources not in the body of the article: e.g. websites, social media, or books in any format referring to the subject covered. Well-researched supporting material and annotated links in box outs increases the likelihood of publication; we cannot emphasize enough the importance of providing practical information that others may use.

Photos, Videos, Graphics. Multimedia is now expected by all those who read about anything related to travel and is a very effective way of engagement. The more visually powerful and sensitive the photos or videos you include, the more the reader will gain a sense of place, people, and culture.

Either journalistic or an experienced conversational writing style. The journalistic style is honestly our preference since we believe a story should tell itself in the 3rd person as much as possible, but if you have refined your conversational style and know how to engage the reader while providing no-nonsense practical information and inspiration, we are open to publishing your submission.

You will find Transition Abroad's guidelines and submission details at:

https://www.transitionsabroad.com/information/writers/writers.shtml

#6

ClearVoice

Overview

Somewhat like a writer's mill, ClearVoice is designed to create a collaborative workspace, which lets companies secure the services of freelance writers.

When you sign up, you are joining a talent network and matched with assignments based on your expertise and rate. Once you add a CV and portfolio, companies will be able to send you work based on your abilities and specified minimum rate. You can also pitch ideas to clients.

With ClearVoice, you set your own rates, which could be anything from 10 cents per word or $1 per word. The lower your rate, the more offers you will get. That said, you can decline any offer if it doesn't suit your schedule, strengths or interests.

FROM THE WEBSITE:

More Than Freelance Writing Jobs. An Entrepreneurial Ladder.

ClearVoice is designed for the future of work. Our Talent Network and collaborative workspace allows freelancers and in-house teams to collaborate seamlessly. Our goal is to help you seize opportunities and deliver your best work — with less hustle and less hassle.

Build Your Personal Brand

If you're serious about freelancing, strengthen your CV Portfolio and use ClearVoice to help grow your business.

Secure Better Jobs

Through your CV, join our Talent Network, where assignments will match your expertise and rate. You also can pitch to clients.

Share Your CV Portfolio

We're constantly improving our CVs (ClearVoice portfolios) so you can better showcase your work and attract more clients.

Set Your Own Rate

You decide what you want to get paid. Set your range to see assignments relevant to you.

Easily Communicate With Clients

In-app messaging allows you to chat with clients at any point in the creation process. This means fewer emails.

Get Paid Quickly

ClearVoice freelancers are paid via PayPal upon assignment approval. Work with the confidence you'll get paid on time.

Get the guidelines and details about the ClearVoice talent network at:

https://www.clearvoice.com/freelance-jobs/

#7

Constant Content

Overview

Constant Content is a good place to make decent money online, whether you're a seasoned professional writer or a new writer just starting out.

With this platform, you can earn one of two ways: You can upload your articles or blog posts and make them available for sale. You set the price, and if someone is interested, they will buy either full or partial rights to the content depending on your preference.

The second method involves the public request area, where businesses ask for specific types of content. You can then write the content and submit it for consideration. If the requester likes it, they will purchase it; if they don't, or someone beats you to the punch, you can always put the piece up for sale to other buyers.

FROM THE WEBSITE:

We Make it Easy for Companies to Find and Hire you!

Constant Content is trusted by thousands of businesses including Uber, Zulily, The Home Depot, Walgreens, Hayneedle, CVS, eBay and others, and is one of the largest and most established platforms for facilitating connections between big brands and you — the best freelance writers online.

Create your profile

Create a professional bio that showcases your writing skills and experience.

Apply for projects

Browse and claim writing jobs that match your interests, expertise and rate.

Connect with brands

Connect with top-brands and build long-term relationships.

Advance your career

Grow your portfolio, build relationships, earn money and advance your career.

Get the guidelines and details about Constant Content at:

https://www.constant-content.com/freelance-writing-jobs.htm

#8

eByline

Overview

eByline is a part of the Izea brand, which connects online influencers with major brands.

If you have a social media profile with a lot of followers, Izea can help you monetize your account by posting about products. If not, that's ok; you can still get paid to write custom content for top brands, publishers, advertisers and ecommerce companies.

To do this, you will need to join the creator marketplace full of freelance opportunities for writers, journalists, photographers, videographers, animators, designers, musicians and composers. Freelancer pay at eByline is all over the chart, but you can expect to make a very good income if you decide to stick with it.

FROM THE WEBSITE:

Monetize your content, creativity, and influence in the largest marketplace of its kind.

You Bring the Passion, We'll Bring the Brands

Create a free profile and get the opportunity to partner with industry-leading food, fashion, beauty, and lifestyle brands. Don't sell your influence short.

Monetize your content, creativity, and influence in the industry's largest social media influencer marketplace. Connect with brands, advertisers, and publishers for sponsorship opportunities to create and share content across your social media accounts in exchange for compensation.

Get paid to create custom content for top brands, advertisers, publishers, and ecommerce companies. Join the creator marketplace full of freelance opportunities for journalists, writers, photographers, videographers, designers, animators, musicians, and composers.

Get the guidelines and details about eByline and the Izea brand at:

https://izea.com/influencers-creators/

#9

nDash

Overview

A relatively new brand, nDash works much like other content providers which seek to earn commission-like fees for linking talent with brands

At this point, the idea should sound familiar: nDash recruits a large pool of writers and makes them available to brands. The businesses then choose the writers for projects and nDash takes a cut of the pay.

If you join the nDash writers pool, you will have the chance to write for thousands of brands of all sizes and industries. You will get paid promptly for each completed assignment, while having a chance to develop real relationships with major brands.

Could this lead to an in-house opportunity with a big company? Perhaps. But, in the meantime, nDash allows you to profit by project. Since you can set your own rates for assignments, it's easy to experiment with numbers to see which rate brings you the most work.

FROM THE WEBSITE:

Elite Writers Wanted

Higher rates, legitimate brands, and six-figure earning potential. Create a free account today.

Great Clients

nDash has thousands of brands of all sizes and industries — and they're all looking for great writers.

Fast Payments

nDash writers get paid with each completed assignment, with no fees taken from your earnings.

Full Transparency

nDash puts you in direct communication with the client so you can build real relationships.

Earning Potential

Aside from paid projects, nDash offers a lifetime royalty for all successful company referrals.

Pitch Top Brands

nDash brands seek the the most talented, experienced and creative writers–not the cheapest. Pitch unique ideas for blog posts, articles and more to showcase your expertise.

Set Your Rates

Forget about starting off with an arbitrary 1-star rating, earning two cents per word. You're better than that (we hope). nDash enables you to set your own rates for assignments.

Open & Transparent

Instead of restricting communication (like other platforms), nDash puts you in direct contact with brands for every assignment so you can build real relationships.

Leverage Your Expertise

Brands on nDash are looking for writers with proven subject matter expertise. Tailor your profile to focus on the topics and categories that interest you most.

Get the guidelines and details about nDash at:

https://www.ndash.co/for-writers

#10

Contently

Overview

Contently is one of the world's largest enterprise content marketing platforms, creative networks and content strategy services.

Through the platform, freelance writers have an opportunity to work with top brands on high-quality projects that pay well. How well? This can vary, but a good project will usually play at least $1 per word.

Once they register with Contently, writers are matched with brands. They can then pitch ideas, submit work and instantly receive payment all in one place. To become eligible for work, writers have to join the network by creating a free portfolio that will showcase their projects and professional expertise.

FROM THE WEBSITE:

Contently's created a platform that allows creatives to showcase their talents in a way that's user-friendly for freelancers. Being able to update a reel or portfolio with only a few clicks and reach new prospective clients makes the process seamless.

Match with clients

Freelancers get assigned to projects based on how well their portfolio matches a client's needs. We work with brands across industries, especially in the areas of finance, healthcare, travel, and enterprise technology.

Collaborate on projects

Once you're on a client's team, you'll be able to pitch to editors and accept assignment briefs. On Contently, you can work on everything from reported stories and case studies to infographics, photoshoots, and
video productions.

Get paid quickly

The moment you submit your work, you'll be credited with payment in your Contently account. As soon as it shows up, you can cash out to your PayPal account.

Keep on going

The more content you pitch, deadlines you meet, and stories you tell (well), the better Contently and our clients get to know you. That means you'll be top-of-mind when the next client comes looking for a talented contributor.

Get the guidelines and details about writing for Contently at:

https://contently.net/

#11

Guideposts

Overview

A pay-per-piece outlet, Guideposts publishes factual stories about subjects who have attained a goal, overcome an obstacle or learned a helpful lesson through their faith.

Writers can earn $250 for typical stories told in a first-person narrative with a spiritual lesson or angle that readers can apply to their lives. Stories can be about the writer or another person.

Payment for stories (approximately 1,500 words) is sent once the story is accepted. Guideposts does not accept essays, sermons or fiction. The publication also almost never uses poetry and will not evaluate book-length material, so keep your story at around 1,500 words.

FROM THE WEBSITE:

Guideposts publishes true stories about people who have attained a goal, surmounted an obstacle or learned a helpful lesson through their faith. A typical story is a first-person narrative with a spiritual point that the reader can apply to his or her own life. The story may be your own or someone else's. Observe the following as you write:

The emphasis should be on one person and told from the vantage point of the individual most deeply affected by the experience. Focus on one specific event rather than an entire life story. Bring only as many people in as are needed to tell the story.

Give all the relevant facts so that the reader can clearly understand what took place. Let the reader feel as if he or she were there, seeing the characters, hearing them talk, feeling what they felt.

Show the positive and specific change in the narrator that occurs as a result of the experience, a message or insight that readers can apply to their own lives.

Payment for full-length stories (about 1,500 words) is made when the story is accepted for publication. Please do not send essays, sermons or fiction. We almost never use poetry and do not evaluate book-length material.

Get the guidelines and details about writing for Guideposts at:

https://www.guideposts.org/writers-guidelines

#12

Chicken Soup for the Soul

Overview

Another pay-per-piece outlet, Chicken Soup for the Soul pays for inspirational, true stories about ordinary people having extraordinary experiences.

The outlet pays $200 for every accepted post. Although you shouldn't expect to make a regular income with this publisher; if your content is accepted, it will be a part of the famous Chicken Soup for the Soul book series.

The outlet has some pretty stringent rules and guidelines, so be sure to thoroughly read over each one before submitting your content.

FROM THE WEBSITE:

Guidelines for a Chicken Soup for the Soul story

1. Tell an exciting, heartwarming or funny story about something that has happened to you or someone you know. Your story should be written in the first person and should be about yourself or someone close to you.

2. Tell your story in a way that will make the reader cry, laugh, get goose bumps or say "Wow!"

3. The story should start "in the action" and draw in the reader. Do not start your story with an introduction about what you are going to say, or end with a concluding paragraph about what you just said.

4. Don't be afraid to speak from the heart. Many people tell personal stories for the first time in our books, and they find it to be a cathartic and productive experience. We do let you use a pen name for your story if you do not want to use your real name.

5. Don't try fancy moves with tenses. Writing in the present tense about something that happened in the past rarely works.

6. Keep your story to 1200 words or less. Tighten, tighten, tighten!

7. Your story must be true. No fiction, no creative writing.

Get the guidelines and details about writing for Chicken Soup for the Soul at:

https://www.chickensoup.com/story-submissions/story-guidelines

#13

Link-Able

Overview

Link-Able allows writers to earn money publishing for a wide range of clients and industries.

The platform matches writers who are able to publish on relevant sites with companies looking to earn mentions, links and traffic to their sites.

Link-Able offers $100 to $750 per piece depending on the sites you either have authorship on or are able to successfully pitch to. Niches include business, marketing, finance, health, sport, tech, retail and more. To earn money with this website, you will need to be able to write good content and get it published at relevant blogs and websites.

FROM THE WEBSITE:

Do you love to guest blog & write articles for the Web? Join Link-able to find link building jobs and multiply your earnings as a freelance writer.

Step 1

You're an exceptionally talented writer who loves to write and can guest blog for websites within your niche.

Step 2

Join Link-able and search for content you can link to in your next article. You'll only find quality results that would make great links.

Step 3

Relevantly add a link to the content you find within your article. Then publish your article on a website you can guest author for.

Step 4

Sit back and relax as you get paid for each link you've added within your article from Link-able!

Earn more with your writing

Freelance writers often don't get paid enough for their work. With Link-able, you can multiply your writing revenue without having to write more! Get paid for simply adding relevant backlinks within your work to sources you choose.

Get paid up to $750 for a single link

You can earn anywhere from $100 to $750 for each link you add – and you can add as many links as you can get. Many of our Content Authors earn over a $1000 in additional revenue just for a single article!

Choose what you want to link to

You can search for and choose only the content you want to link to – and then get paid for it! On Link-able, we only allow websites with high-quality content, so you always have great choices to link to.

Work with topics you're already working on

There's no need to write about a topic you don't want to. Simply search on Link-able to find great content you can link to that's related to the topic you're already writing.

Grow your writing portfolio & career

Link-able encourages freelance writers to go out and build a name for yourself. We want you to contribute and publish your work on new places. With Link-able, you can grow your author portfolio and get paid for writing quality articles you'll be proud to share on your portfolio.

Earn more for your writing today

Don't miss out from reaching your true earning potential as a writer. Start boosting your earnings and signup as a Content Author on Link-able today!

Get the guidelines and details about writing for Link-Able at:

https://link-able.com/content-authors/

#14

Funds for Writers

Overview

FundsforWriters pays for practical articles aimed at helping writers get paid for their writing.

They have a preference for success stories, but informative pieces sell well too as long as they are well-researchers.

You can expect to make from $45 to $50 per article, depending on whether you want to be paid via Paypal or by check. Articles are usually accepted within a week of submission.

FROM THE WEBSITE:

Freelance Submission Process for FundsforWriters

Articles should fall between 500 and 600 words. Each FundsforWriters newsletter lists only one article – short and sweet and to the point. So make each word count. MAKE YOUR WRITING TIGHT. Watch the passive voice. Give it a beginning, middle, and ending. A list of links is not an article.

IT MUST BE ABOUT EARNING A LIVING AS A WRITER.

We do NOT want stories about…

how to write
how to develop plot, characters or settings
topics that cannot relate in some manner to making more money as a writer
general or theoretical anything without solid examples and resources

We DO want…

ideas on breaking into a particular writing market (but try to avoid one vendor/publication)
pointers on winning writing contests
unique ways to develop an income with words
success stories about being a writer with ideas for others
profitable business practices related to writing

seasonal material affiliated with particular markets

grant success stories

nonprofit partnerships for writers

unique markets for writers

unusual writing income ideas

anything to help a writer make a dollar penning words

a dash of humor, if possible; a positive note and a happy ending

if you suggest an idea, make sure you have proof it works through your own experience or interviews with others

Payment:

Via PayPal – $50 for unpublished original articles; $15 for reprints.

Via check – We rarely pay via check and never outside the US.

Get the guidelines and details about writing for Funds for Writers at:

https://fundsforwriters.com/submissions/

#15

eCommerce Insiders

64

Overview

eCommerce Insiders pays a good rate for articles about online commerce and retail.

You can expect to earn between $75 and $150 for 400- to 600-word articles, which comes out to a very competitive pay-per-word rate.

You will need to have some specific ecommerce experience, or experience in a field that is relevant in some way to ecommerce.

FROM THE WEBSITE:

eCommerce Insiders writers are ecommerce subject matter experts. As providers to the online retail industry or retailers themselves, their perspective is shaped by direct experience.

Our writers contribute articles adhering to the following guidelines:

1. Retail-Focused
Content must be angled toward online retailers and fit into one categories/subcategories in the site navigation menu above.

2. Commentary or Educational
Content should either be educational with "how to" tips and tactics, or commentary on industry news or trends. We tolerate no explicit sales/marketing persuasion for your business in the article itself. We reserve the right to edit content and remove any promotional links before publication.

Every writer is given an "author box" which displays at the article conclusion. Links are permitted in this section which typically includes content such as your bio, company background, and a single offer.

Payment

We pay for high quality, exclusive, original content according to the following schedule:

$75 for every article from 400-600 words
$125 for every article >600 words
$150 for every article 600+ words

We pay writers once per month for the preceding month's published articles. Articles that don't meet our editorial guidelines of retail-focused, high quality, exclusive, original content will be rejected without pay.

Get the guidelines and details about writing for eCommerce Insiders at:

https://ecommerceinsiders.com/write/

#16

Upwork

Overview

The world's largest freelancer marketplace, Upwork resulted from the merger between oDesk and eLance a few years ago.

The platform makes it easy for writers at every skill level to capitalize on the opportunity to work online. Upwork's marketplace is controlled by support vs. demand, and the company has the market cornered so the majority of respectable writing jobs flow this way.

If you'd like to deal with clients privately, Upwork is the place to do it. You'll have to pay a percentage of your earnings to Upwork, but this won't stop you from earning thousands of dollars if you leverage the platform efficiently.

FROM THE WEBSITE:

Find the best freelance jobs

Work with a purpose. And a smile.

COME MAKE HISTORY

Help bring online work to every corner of the world.

DO STUFF YOU'RE PROUD OF

Be part of a fun and passionate crew reinventing an industry. Along the way you'll draw a nice paycheck and work on projects that truly matter.

WHISTLE WHILE YOU WORK

Enjoy a healthy work/life balance, with great perks from free lunches and fun afternoon social activities to work-from-home Wednesdays.

Get the guidelines and details about writing through Upwork at:

https://www.upwork.com/hire/writers/

#17

Scripted

Overview

Scripted gives writers immediate access to corporate clients who pay up to 10 cents per word.

To gain access, however, you need to get approved as a Scripted writer. This means you will need to be able to show off your talent through writing samples and/or a portfolio.

Since they get contracts from big-name corporations such as eBay, Wal-Mart and Sportchek, scripted is a great place to gain experience and build up your portfolio. When things are busy, you'll see enough work to earn $5,000 or more in a single month. Since things can slow down, however, you should look to supplement your workflow through another platform or part-time job

FROM THE WEBSITE:

Wondering How to Become a Freelance Writer?

Apply to become a freelance writer on Scripted. Scripted's mission is to pair the best writers with the best clients. Scripted writers earn an average of over ten cents per word and fully control their pricing and workload.

How It Works

Scripted makes earning good money as a freelance writer simple and easy

Work Directly with Businesses

Propose jobs directly to customers. Build relationships with customers through in-app messaging.

Write in Any Industry

New projects are available every day. Propose jobs to a wide variety of project topics.

Payment is Guaranteed

Get paid automatically 15 days after your job is accepted. Qualify for partial payment on any rejected job.

Set Your Own Prices

Set your own prices and earn a higher rate on job requests and when you propose jobs. Minimum pricing on each job ensures all writers earn a fair wage.

Create a Portfolio

Host samples of your work in your Scripted profile. Build out your profile and get customers to come to you.

Make Your Own Schedule

Control your workload and set your own hours. Take a vacation whenever you want.

Work from Anywhere

You're free to work anywhere with an Internet connection. Scripted currently supports writers that live in 20+ countries.

Get the guidelines and details about writing through Scripted at:

https://www.scripted.com/become-a-scripted-writer

#18

Zerys

Why Join the Zerys Writer Network

- ✔ Get started for free - no monthly fees or bid credits required
- ✔ Get notified when new jobs are posted that match your profile
- ✔ Develop long term relationships with clients and build a steady source of work

| Read Writer FAQs | Browse Writer Blog |

Thank you for your interest in becoming a writer for Zerys!

We are currently not accepting new applications at this time. If you'd like to be notified when we

Overview

One of the lesser-known writing platforms, Zerys provides regular work if you check it often.

You will find some amazing earning opportunities if you establish yourself with a quality reputation. You will need to do good work, however, because assignments are handed out based on quality scores from clients.

At Zerys, you can set your own rate, and many top-level clients pay at least 7 cents a word. You can also apply for editing assignments that pay very well if your writing feedback holds strong for a while.

FROM THE WEBSITE:

Why Join the Zerys Writer Network

Get started for free - No monthly fees or bid credits required

Get notified when new jobs are posted that match your profile

Develop long-term relationships with clients and build a steady source of work

Is Zerys an employer?

No. Zerys is an online content production platform that connects freelance writers and editors to businesses that are looking for online content. Zerys is only a software platform and does not employ or contract its users. Writers and editors in the Zerys platform are considered their own self-employed entities, and are referred to as Freelance Service Providers, because they provide content services to clients who use the Zerys platform.

What is my Direct Assign pay rate?

Your Direct Assign rate is the rate that you want to net out for direct assignments. It is not the actual Client Rate, which will be 30% more than your Direct Assign rate to account for our commission.

If a client assigns a job to you directly, unless they request a different rate and you agree to that rate, this is the rate that the client will pay to you. Determine the per-word rate that you would like to work for, based on your skill level and experience.

Keep in mind that any job taken from any job board will be paid at the rate at which it was posted. You will not be paid your Direct Assign rate for job board jobs unless the rates for those jobs happen to match your rate.

Get the guidelines and details about writing through Zerys at:

https://www.zerys.com/writers

#19

Content Gather

Overview

Content Gather is a content writing platform that connects writers with website owners who need content (blog posts, articles, press releases, product reviews, product descriptions, how-tos, tutorials and more).

The service gives writers a way to earn money doing what they love and provides website owners with unique, informative content.

Content Gather pays up to 10 cents per word once you have elite status. To gain this status, register on the site, upload a few articles and send an email saying, "please upgrade me."

FROM THE WEBSITE:

A content writing service offering a platform to connect writers with website owners who need content (articles, blog posts, press releases, product descriptions, product reviews, how-tos, tutorials, and more). Writers have a platform to earn money doing what they enjoy and website owners receive content exactly as they want.

Lightning Fast Payment

Writers, request payment whenever you want and receive your money within 24 hours, guaranteed. On your schedule, not ours.

Writers, Get Paid Before You Sell!

You don't have to wait weeks or months to receive payment for your pre-written article. If you're a Silver level writer, you'll receive a percentage of your asking price as soon as your pre-written article is approved, before it even sells! Then when it does sell, you'll receive the rest as well.

Get the guidelines and details about writing for Content Gather at:

https://contentgather.com

#20

iWriter

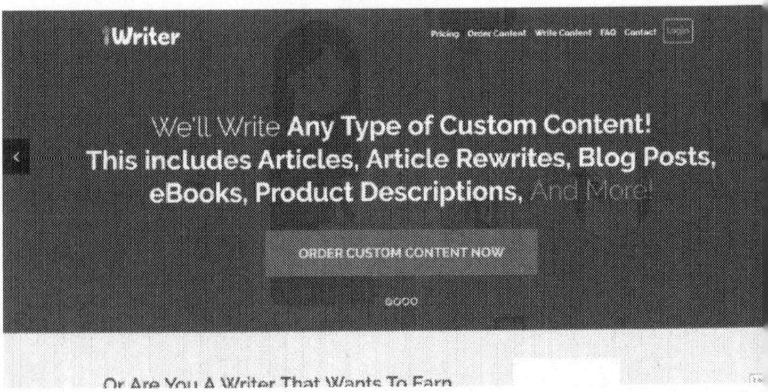
iWriter
Pricing Order Content Write Content FAQ Contact Login
We'll Write Any Type of Custom Content!
This includes Articles, Article Rewrites, Blog Posts,
eBooks, Product Descriptions, And More!
ORDER CUSTOM CONTENT NOW

Overview

iWriter is a good place to supplement your writing work, but it does have its problems.

If you do at least 40 posts without having your quality score drop under 4.85 out of 5, you will be able to see all the higher-paying open Elite Plus jobs. If your score is over 4.6, you can still find a fair number of Elite level assignments on here.

In the end, however, you will probably struggle to make more than $500 a month off iWriter, so try to view it as a way to build your portfolio and/or fill out your workflow.

FROM THE WEBSITE:

iWriter is the fastest, easiest and most reliable way to have content written for your website. You'll be able to post a project and 1000s of freelance writers from across the globe will have instant access to write your content quickly, professionally, and affordably.

Are You A Writer That Wants to Earn Money Writing For iWriter?

Build Your Own Client Base.

Earn Up To $80 Per 500 Words Once Promoted Up The Ranks.

Write As Much Or As Little As You Want Each Day.

Choose The Topics That Best Match Your Background.

Get the guidelines and details about writing through iWriter at:

https://www.iwriter.com/writer-application

#21

HireWriters

Overview

A lower-paying site for less experienced writers, HireWriters is a decent option if you just need to make a few bucks.

Don't expect to break the bank. If you take an assignment, the goal would be to complete it quickly, since most are just basic blog posts for SEO purposes.

If you do it right and type fast, you can make some spare money; however, you should understand that this platform is better suited for younger writers with no experience and those with English language issues, who need to build their portfolios and gain some online writing experience.

FROM THE WEBSITE:

Sign up and get paid to write

If English is your first language, join HireWriters.com today for FREE and you will have access to HUNDREDS of paid writing jobs. Clients post writing assignments and you can then accept the job and get paid when you complete it!

Your membership is 100% FREE

- Get paid up to $20 per article you write once you become established on HireWriters.com.
- Work and earn as much as you want!
- Write about the topics you want
- Get bonus payments from clients when you do a good job
- Complete other types of jobs such as: proofreading, research, ideas and article rewriting
- Get paid every week on Friday

Get the guidelines and details about writing through HireWriters at:

https://www.hirewriters.com/signup/writer

#22

CopyPress

Overview

CopyPress is a unique writing platform that doesn't function like the traditional writer's mill.

Instead of merely throwing work in front of writers, CopyPress scouts for great writing talent and matches people to contracts.

In addition to functioning as a paid writing site, CopyPress is a network where writers to interact. There are many writers who have been matched with corporate clients and now earn $20 to $60 an hour, all thanks to their free CopyPress membership.

FROM THE WEBSITE:

What We Do

Creating things is a unifying passion at CopyPress. Since 2009, we've fed that passion by building software, products, and services that help creatives and advertisers do the same.

We built a Community where writers, designers, and developers can create their own micro-businesses centered around their passion. CopyPress and our proprietary software is the conduit for this community and our clients to create engaging campaigns with compelling content.

Our ability to connect our large community of trained creatives with clients ranging from mid-market companies to digital agencies and Fortune 500 organizations allows us to do what we love: build tools that enable both creatives and advertisers to scale, promote, and most importantly, create.

You'll need to contact CopyPress and request a screening invitation.

https://www.copypress.com/contact-us/

#23

Crowd Content

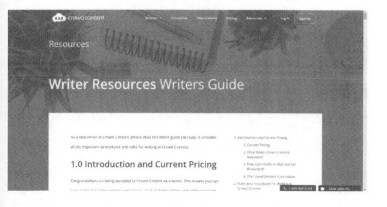

Overview

Crowd Content is a scalable content marketplace for agencies, brands and retailers.

From a writer's point of view, the platform offers a very diverse pay scale, which runs from a few cents per word up to $1.75 per word.

If you accept a lot of jobs and these jobs are reviewed positively, you will be matched with higher paying gigs.

FROM THE WEBSITE:

Access freelance content writing jobs, start claiming orders and writing content for Crowd Content clients. Best of all, you're going to get paid for every word you write!

What Makes Crowd Content Awesome?

You'll notice quickly that Crowd Content is a bit different than other writing companies out there. That's because we've added some gamification into the mix.

What's gamification, you ask? Currently, Wikipedia says:

Gamification is the use of game-thinking and game mechanics in a non-game context in order to engage users and solve problems. Gamification is used in applications and processes to improve user engagement, ROI, data quality, timeliness, and learning.

In other words, we're tracking a few key performance metrics for every writer in our system. Writers who perform well are rewarded. Pretty simple, right?

When you sign in to your writer account, click on your profile image in the top right corner. This is where you can see your current performance levels at any time.

Get the guidelines and details about writing for Crowd Content at:

https://www.crowdcontent.com/resources/writer/guide/

#24

TextBroker

Overview

Since 2005, Textbroker has been one of the leading providers of unique, custom content.

It's one of the very first content mills, and it hasn't changed a whole lot over time. If you are just starting out, Textbroker gives you access to thousands of diverse writing opportunities for a wide array of topics. You can choose when and how much content you write, and there is no limit to how much you can earn.

Unfortunately, TextBroker doesn't pay very well until you level up by writing a specified amount of well-received content. Even then, you won't be making much more than 5 cents per word. Still, it's a good place to get experience or make some extra money if you don't have a very substantial writing portfolio.

FROM THE WEBSITE:

Earn money to write content

Is writing your passion? Then Textbroker is the right place for you. Since 2005, Textbroker is the leading provider of unique, custom content. Thousands of registered authors and customers from around the globe execute more than 100,000 content orders through Textbroker every month. Our clients, including publicly traded corporations, small business owners, e-commerce websites, social media communities, and publishing houses, require a broad variety of content.

If you are just starting out or are an experienced professional, Textbroker gives you access to thousands of writing opportunities for each topic. Choose when and how much content you write – there is no limit to how much you can earn.

Why Write for Textbroker

Free of charge, flexible time management, and reliable payment: Read here why it pays to become a Textbroker author.

How Textbroker Works

Whether you are a beginner or an experienced professional, Textbroker has the right project for every author. Receive your first order in just a few simple steps.

Payment

Textbroker offers several payment options. The better your content, the more you can earn. Find out more here.

Writing Resources

We are vested in your success. We give feedback to help you refine your skills and access to our blog that includes grammar tips, tutorials, and videos.

Get the guidelines and details about writing for Textbroker at:

https://www.textbroker.com/authors

#25

The Content Authority

99

Overview

The Content Authority is another content writing platform that connects writers with website owners who need blog posts, articles, press releases, product reviews, product descriptions, etc.

Pay varies, with the lowest starting at less than one cent per word and the highest at 3 cents per word. Once you hit $25 in your account, you can cash in and get paid via PayPal.

This is another place you should only choose if you need experience, have trouble with English, just want to make a few extra dollars or don't have a very substantial writing portfolio.

FROM THE WEBSITE:

The Content Authority is a young, dynamic company with humble beginnings and a major mission. Our primary goal is to supply existing businesses and web entrepreneurs with relevant content that will add value to their websites. With a focus on providing high quality for less money, our objective is to give your business the edge it needs to succeed in a highly competitive market. Founded in 2009 on the principles of excellent customer support and exceptional service, combined with great value, The Content Authority collaborates with some of the most creatively charged writers on the planet.

Writer Requirements

You can read and comprehend English.

You can write formal articles using proper English grammar at a high school level.

You have the ability to do accurate research about a variety of topics dependent on the requirements of our clients.

You are able to follow the instructions of our clients as well as the requirements posted by The Content Authority.

You are capable and willing to write articles within specified deadlines.

You are able to be paid through PayPal.

You are willing to accept critiques about your work from both Clients and The Content Authority staff.

Get the guidelines and details about writing for The Content Authority at:

https://thecontentauthority.com/create-an-account/application-to-write

#26

Writers Weekly

ANGELA'S DESK   ARTICLES   HOME OFFICE   SUCCESS STORY   WHISPERS & WARNINGS   LETTERS & COMMENTS

ASK THE EXPERT   PAYING MARKETS & JOBS   24-HOUR SHORT STORY CONTEST!   POD SECRETS REVEALED

Angela's Desk

WHAT ARE THEY
REALLY HIDING?
One HUGE Red Flag
To Watch Out For
When Choosing a
Publisher!
July 24th, 2019

Some firms claim to "pay half of the
author's publishing fees - but are they
really doing that? Those thousand
dollars to MORE than enough to pay

Comments

- Richard Hoy on Using
  a package to buy
  Books...but NOT in the
  way you expect to
  ripFeedYour
  DeadBook.com

- Av Angela Hoy -
  Publisher of
  WritersWeekly.com on
  I Caught a Stupid of
  Spammer

Trivia Question!

Writers Weekly Trivia Question For
9/7/2019
July 24, 2019 - 11 am

Overview

Writers Weekly is an online publication that is distributed to paying subscribers.

They seek articles that give freelance writers insight into how they can make more money writing.

It's best to submit something with a unique angle, since the vast majority of rejections center on topics that have already received too much exposure in the industry.

With Writers Weekly, you will be paid anything from $40 to $60 for approved articles.

FROM THE WEBSITE:

WritersWeekly.com focuses on "selling" the written word. We do not seek articles on how to write. Rather, we seek articles on how to make more money doing what you love....writing! We are also interested in other forms of home-based businesses and self-employment that may result from writing, such as self-publishing, corporate writing, ghostwriting, etc. All ideas that help writers support themselves performing the work they love are warmly welcomed.

Other topics of interest: Corporate writing, writing for markets of a specific genre (with links to those markets' guidelines, and information on how much they pay), unique book marketing ideas, and anything that isn't already done-to-death in the industry. The vast majority of rejections we send out are for queries that are on topics that have already received too much exposure in the industry, or already covered by us.

We receive a lot of queries with misspelled words, incorrect punctuation, missing punctuation, capitalization errors, and on topics that aren't even remotely related to writing or publishing at all. If we receive a query about pets, religion, and other things completely unrelated to our genre, we will not respond. We aren't trying to be rude but, if a writer can't be bothered to even read the name of our publication to see the genre we cover, we can't be bothered to respond to that query. We hope you understand.

We pay in U.S. Dollars.

FEATURES: We are seeking articles on various ways writers can make money from their writing (i.e. unique assignments, corporate services, self publishing, marketing and networking advice, alternative products and services that writers can pursue and sell). We also seek articles on how authors can successfully market their books to the public, as well as warnings about industry scams or about businesses may not necessarily be scams, but that may be a waste of money for writers and authors. See past Features HERE.

FREELANCE SUCCESS STORIES: "In each issue, we publish a freelance success story, and pay $40 for first rights to these. Success stories average 400 words. If you'd like to share your freelance success story with us, please send a query first using the contact info. provided above. Freelance success stories should, through your personal story, offer advice to other writers on how they, too, can succeed doing what you did. Please note we do not publish "one-shot" success stories – meaning we don't publish stories on how a writer sold one story to one publication. We prefer to focus on actions the writer took to become a successful freelancer or a successful author. Please note that we do not publish success stories that detail the writer writing for free, or almost-free (like with content mills), nor stories about writers who post articles on website that pay a commission based on advertising generated on those page (because those deals are usually a horrible deal for writers). Our readers need to feed their families with their writing and we strongly discourage writing for free because this ultimately hurts all writers by making publishers think that quality writing can be obtained for free. We encourage writers to submit a generous bio to run under their success story where they can advertise their freelance writing service, book, etc. This is over and above the 400-word count." See past Success Stories HERE.

PAYMENT INFO – For features: Pays $60 for around 600 words. For success stories: Pays $40 for around 400 words. First rights for articles. Submit query and credits by e-mail.

Get the guidelines and details about writing for Writers Weekly at:

https://writersweekly.com/writersweekly-com-writers-guidelines

#27

Listverse

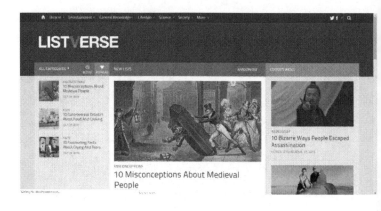

Overview

Listverse will pay for interesting list articles about anything, as long as the topic is unusual, unique or interesting.

The site will pay you $100 for every approved list, and the editors generally want articles to be around 1,500 words and feature at least 10 items.

If you have a Twitter account, blog or a book you want to promote, mention it in the submissions form, and Listverse will promote it at the bottom of your list.

FROM THE WEBSITE:

Do you want to earn money online? Listverse was built on the efforts of readers just like you. Readers who didn't have any experience as writers but decided to put a list together and send it in.

So here is the deal: We will pay you $100 for your efforts. You don't need to be an expert—you just need to have English equal to that of a native speaker, a sense of humor, and a love for things unusual or interesting.

It works like this: You write your list (10 items per list minimum), you send it in, we reply and say "Great—we'll publish it" and send you $100 by PayPal (don't have an account? just make one—it's easy and free); or we reply and say "Sorry—it isn't the sort of thing our readers will love—give it another shot." Just remember, your list should be at least one or two paragraphs per entry.

Either way you win—your list will be read by us and reviewed, and if it's amazing it will appear on the front page of Listverse to be read by millions of people a month!

We can not accept lists from writers who do not have a PayPal account; this is non-negotiable. If PayPal doesn't support your country, please don't request alternative methods of payment.

The rules are really pretty simple. As long as your list (and we do mean yours—don't steal other people's stuff) is one or two paragraphs per item you can choose any topic you like. We also need you to link to reputable sources (see Section 7 of our author guide for more details) so we can verify the facts of what you're saying. Just remember—if it's good enough to publish (by our standards) you get 100 bucks—simple as that.

Get the guidelines and details about writing for Listverse at:

https://listverse.com/write-get-paid/

#28

Back to College®

Overview

Back to College® is a news and information resource for adult re-entry students pursuing advanced or professional development degrees.

They are looking for articles about education for older students. Think on campus and online education, obtaining financial aid, finding the right program, graduate school, etc.

Back to College® pays between $75 and $135 per article, and payment is made by check or via Paypal 30 days after an accepted article has been published.

FROM THE WEBSITE:

Compensation

Feature Articles: Payment is $55+ for original feature articles ($27.50+ for reprints and derivatives), approximately 1,000 - 1,500+ words in length (compensation is determined by depth). Payment is rendered by check or PayPal 30 days after publication and receipt of invoice. (You can choose method of payment. Payment by check involves a $5 administrative and mailing fee).

Please note: Articles will not be accepted for payment if they may be considered promotional in nature, provide information about a Web site, product, or service, or are written for SEO purposes.

Publishing Terms and Conditions

By submitting articles for publication on Back to College®, you grant WD Communications LLC exclusive first-serial rights to the articles for one year, with non-exclusive serial rights thereafter (including the right to archive the article online on an indefinite basis), and the world-wide, royalty free and non-exclusive license to use, distribute, reproduce, publish, and incorporate the article (in whole or in part) in any ancilliary or subsidiary product or reprint.

By submitting an article, you represent that you are its sole author or creator, or that you are submitting it with the permission of its author or creator who has agreed to these terms and conditions. You also grant WD Communications LLC permission to publish your photo in any publication or Web site in relation to your article. WD Communications LLC reserves the right to edit articles for grammar and style. Author will receive a byline and photo with a short summary of biographical information.

Get the guidelines and details about writing for Back to College® at:

http://www.back2college.com/guide.htm

#29

Dollar Stretcher

Subscribe ▾   Money Tools ▾   Book Shop

How Anyone Can Win the Lottery

Most of us play the lottery occasionally, and some play regularly. But how many of us really win anything? Here's the secret to how anyone can win the lottery. Yes, even you!

🔘 Are you a victim of the 'sunken cost fallacy'?

🔘 How do I make my overspending spouse a tightwad?

🔘 Frugal? Or just plain cheap?

🔘 You're 55+ and didn't save enough for retirement
   edenofinances.com

🔘 5 radical cost-cutting tips to reduce the tightest budget

🔘 Do you need to put yourself in financial prison?
   From the Editor's Desk

10 Tools to Get the Best Deals on Membership Programs

So many companies have membership programs now. It is a tactic retailers use to gain customer loyalty by offering

Overview

Dollar Stretcher pays for articles that help people save time and money.

The publication generally wants in-depth articles with practical ideas that people can use to help them stretch their dollars.

For every article accepted at The Dollar Stretcher, you will be paid $0.10 per word. This means you will get $100 for a 1000-word article, and $500 for a 5,000-word article.

FROM THE WEBSITE:

Who We Are

The Dollar Stretcher is a group of publications dedicated to "Living Better...for Less". The goal is to provide readers with ways to help them save time and money. Occasionally we will also include material on ways to make money at home.

The bi-monthly print version of the newsletter made it's debut in January 1998. We offer it with different covers and lengths for use by private organizations. So, in effect we're creating more than one newsletter with the same content. Our online newsletters go out weekly with a circulation of 200,000. Our web site serves over 1 million page views each month. Our index pages are updated daily, but most articles are featured (i.e. linked from the index page) for 7 days.

In addition we promote articles on Facebook, Twitter (@dollarstretch), and other social media to increase exposure.

The site is crawled regularly by the search engines and nearly half of our traffic comes from search. So any original content could draw search engine attention.

What We're Looking For

We're looking for specific ways to help people save time and money. In depth articles with practical ideas that people can employ to help them stretch their dollars.

We do not want another submission on "8 ways to save on groceries." Rather query us on something more specific. We prefer articles that include relevant quotes from experts in the field being discussed or statistics that can help the reader know more about the topic. We're getting away from "here's what I learned about..." type of articles.

Get the guidelines and details about writing for Dollar Stretcher at:

https://www.stretcher.com/menu/writers.cfm

#30

Content Divas

Overview

Content Divas offers a diversity of writing projects for approved writers.

This includes blog content, articles, reports or even full-fledged books. Pay will vary based on the project. You will also work through a Basecamp project management platform once approved.

Unfortunately, Content Divas only accepts new writers every so often, so you will have to keep a watchful eye for when applications open up.

FROM THE WEBSITE:

The Basics of Working with Content Divas
Here are a few other things you might want to
be aware of before you spend your time writing and
submitting content for review.

- All staff members are independent
  contractors. We will not withhold taxes.

- Our company is not set up for writers that just
  want to work now and then. When we look at
  how many writers we have on staff, this helps
  us determine how much work we can take on.
  So if you're not looking to work regularly,
  this will not be a good fit for you.

- You will have to provide us with your name,
  address, and phone number.

- You will be asked to sign an NDA to protect
  our client's content and our own, as well as a
  contract with our company. Note: The
  contract does not require you to work for us
  for any specific amount of time, and it does
  not require you to work ONLY for us. You are
  welcome to continue freelancing outside of
  Content Divas. The contract is to establish an
  agreement that you are being hired as a "ghost
  writer" and you don't retain rights to the
  content that you are paid to write for the
  clients. It also contains a non-compete

agreement stating you won't create a competing outsourcing company, etc. These are all standard protections, nothing that would bind a writer to work for us, etc.

Get the guidelines and details about writing for Content Divas at:

https://contentdivas.com/write-for-content-divas/

#31

Sitepoint

Overview

Sitepoint pays for content that is instructive, technical, well-written and innovative.

Sitepoint writers are typically web professionals with a passion for design and development. The site has amassed more than 10 million readers per month and produced more than 10,000 articles and books.

They are always looking for new writers to join their contributor pool. Pay varies, but you can expect to make above-industry rates for quality articles about CSS, JavaScript, PHP, Ruby, Mobile development, UX, Design and HTML.

FROM THE WEBSITE:

We always welcome having new writers join our contributor pool. They must have a strong desire to produce quality content with actionable advice that readers can apply in their own projects.

In return, we pay our writers above industry rates for their work.

What kind of content do we publish?

Each month, we produce a hub. We focus our energies on one topic, creating content across articles and books that provide readers with a linear path to competency in that skill. In recent months, we've created hubs covering React, web performance, and analytics.

In future months, we'll be looking at subjects like Node, Angular, UX prototyping and Vue. We add to our list of planned hubs as each quarter progresses.

Generally, the content required for each hub is determined in advance by the hub editor, and assigned to available authors. We welcome ideas from authors as hubs enter their planning phase, but pitching specific article ideas no longer forms a core part of our editorial process.

Get the guidelines and details about writing for Sitepoint at:

https://www.sitepoint.com/write-for-us/

#32

IncomeDiary

Overview

IncomeDiary is another writing outlet for developers.

The site pays $50-$200 for articles about making money online, including affiliate sales, SEO and traffic generation.

You can write about creating awesome websites, traffic generation, social media or online income, but your article needs to be of the highest standard.

FROM THE WEBSITE:

If you are an expert at anything to do with: Creating awesome websites, driving traffic, social media or making money online, we would love you to write for us.

We are currently looking for an expert in search engine optimization to write an in depth blog post about keyword research using either Ahref or SemRush. Contact us with a quote (Please include examples of previous writing on SEO – our Budget: $200 – $500).

How Much Do We Pay?

If you are a professional writer and would like to be paid, please let us know when you submit your article for review – including your usual fee.

We do pay up to $200 for worthy articles of the highest standard – but we emphasize that your article needs to be of the highest standard and genuinely of interest to our audience.

Get the guidelines and details about writing for IncomeDiary at:

https://www.incomediary.com/write-for-incomediary

#33

Stork Guide

BABY GEAR   BABY   TODDLER   YOUR BODY   LAUGH   MONEY

Write for us

Overview

Stork Guide publishes content that helps expectant moms and new moms with newborns and toddlers.

That said, the site welcomes contributors from all walks of life, not just moms. If you can offer good content relating to one of their categories, they will pay you to write for them.

You can expect to make $50-plus per piece, depending on the length and style of content. Each post will also include your byline with a link to your website.

FROM THE WEBSITE:

As a hub for new moms, we want to publish content that helps moms with children from newborn up to toddlers and of course, expectant moms. A lot of our readers are first time moms, so if you have content that is really helpful to a first-time mom, that's a bonus!

We welcome contributors from all walks of life, not just moms. If you're an expert in one of our categories that can help moms we want to hear from you too.

Types of posts we accept

Original feature posts

How tos, guides, tips, experiences etc. that are engaging, relatable super helpful and specific. Minimum 700 words.
Payment: $50+ depending on the length and style of content.
Includes byline with link to your website.

Short posts

These are short (around 300 words), entertaining posts or lists that don't require a lot of writing such as this one http://storkguide.com/5-baby-shower-gifts-for-parents-with-a-sense-of-humor/.
Currently unpaid. Includes byline with link to your website.

Syndicated content

- Content that has already been published on your own blog or another website that would also be a good fit for our readers.
- Unpaid. Includes byline with link to your website.

Get the guidelines and details about writing for Stork Guide at:

http://storkguide.com/write-for-us/

#34

Freedom with Writing

Freedom With Writing Submission Guidelines

Thank you for your interest in writing for Freedom With Writing.

Our primary focus is getting writers paid for their writing. We do that by sending writers lists of publishers that pay.

For example, 7 Magazines that Pay Writers $150 (or More).

We also publish the occasional how-to article geared at helping writers learn an important skill for getting paid. (These are less likely to be published.)

I am currently seeking case studies from freelance writers. I want real-world studies about how you got a lucrative freelance writing job, including details about how you landed the gig, sample pitch letters and/or communication with clients, and exact dollar amounts. This will be an example for other writers to follow. Email submissions@freedomwithwriting.com with "Case Study" in the subject line. Pay starts at $50.

We also publish lists of upcoming writing contests.

We only feature publishers that pay writers. We never feature any publisher that requires submission fees.

- We pay $30 to $150 for list articles, depending on length. Lists usually range from 7 publishers up to 50.
- We pay $30 to $150 for how-to articles, essays, and other content. These articles should include real-world examples, including amounts earned. We are especially interested in case studies of how you got a good writing gig. Here is an example, and another example.

We also publish eBooks for writers, which are periodically given away completely free to our audience, as well as published on the Amazon Kindle. We pay a flat rate for these eBooks. They're generally around 10,000

135

Overview

Freedom with Writing will send you writing jobs and articles so you can find steady work.

That said, the site will also pay for content. Freedom with Writing pays up to $100 for lists of paying publishers.

They also pay $500 for short eBooks, so there is an option for longer-form content, too.

FROM THE WEBSITE:

Our primary focus is getting writers paid for their writing. We do that by sending writers lists of publishers that pay, how-to articles that are extremely focused on real-world ways to get paid to write, and case studies from successful freelance writers

We only feature publishers that pay writers. We never feature any publisher that requires submission fees.

We pay $30 to $100 for list articles, depending on length. Lists usually range from 7 publishers up to 50. If you would like to submit a list of publishers, please query first. We prefer to only list publishers that have not been listed previously in our newsletter or website. We are moving towards paying for individual listings added to our database, as opposed to list articles directly.

We pay $30 to $150 for how-to articles, essays, and other content. These articles should include real-world examples, including amounts earned. We are especially interested in case studies of how you got a good writing gig. Here is an example, and another example.

We also publish eBooks for writers, which are generally given away completely free to our audience, as well as published on the Amazon Kindle. We pay a flat rate for these eBooks. They're generally around 10,000 words. Pay starts at $500. See the No B.S.

Guide to Freelance Writing and The Paid and Published Writer.

We are currently interested in case studies about clients that have paid over $1,000. See this example, and this example.

Get the guidelines and details about writing for Freedom with Writing at:

http://www.freedomwithwriting.com/freedom/freedom-with-writing-submission-guidelines/

#35

Online Writing Jobs

Overview

Formerly known as QualityGal, Online Writing Jobs has been paying writers for content since 2006.

The platform uses a per-project, rubric-driven pay scale, and final payment relates to the grade indicated by the rubric.

With that said, average payout ranges from $10 to $27 per project, depending on the project specs.

FROM THE WEBSITE:

Online Writing Jobs has been around since 2006, previously branded as QualityGal. We rebranded because this very lovely and relevant domain was available; it was time for a facelift (and that lift has held up quite well, if we do say so ourselves!), and nobody (of repute) searches for QualityGal or its variants.

We are limited to U.S.-based writers who can provide the required documentation. See step #3.

Writers can invoice at will, and we pay weekly via PayPal or check.

We use a per-project, rubric-driven pay scale, and final payment is linked to the grade indicated by the rubric. Average payout ranges between $27 and $10 per project, depending on the project specs.

Showcase your skills and niche knowledge with additional direct-offer dedicated writing opportunities.

Get the guidelines and details about writing for Online Writing Jobs at:

https://www.onlinewritingjobs.com/new-general-signup/

ADDITIONAL RESOURCES

If you're looking for some great insight and guidance to help kickstart a new writing career or take your existing career to the next level, the following resources are highly recommended. **(All available at Amazon for Kindle and in print.)**

1) *How to Make a Living as a Writer*

by James Scott Bell

It's the best time on Earth to be a writer

More writers are making money today than at any other time in history. For centuries few have been able to support themselves from the quill or the keyboard alone.

Not anymore. With the rise of ebooks and indie publishing there are now more opportunities than ever for writers to generate substantial income from their work. And there is still a traditional publishing industry that needs new talent to keep growing.

In How to Make a Living as a Writer, you'll learn the secrets of writing for profit and increasing your chances of making a living wage from your work. Here are some of the subjects covered:

- The 7 Secrets of Writing Success
- The 8 Essentials of Your Writing Business
- How to Reach Your Goals
- Keys to a Winning System
- How to Stay Relentless
- Unlocking Your Creativity
- How to Write More, Faster
- Comparing Traditional and Self-Publishing
- How to Go Traditional
- How to Go Indie
- How to Form Multiple Streams of Writing Income
- How to Write a Novel in a Month
- How to Choose Non-Fiction Subjects
- How to Keep a Positive Mental Attitude
- Resources for Further Study

And much more, all to help you write what you love and earn what you're worth.

James Scott Bell has made a living as a writer for nearly two decades, and shares with you everything he knows about the best practices for turning your writing dream into a reality.

2) *The Scribe Method: The Best Way to Write and Publish Your Non-Fiction Book*

by Tucker Max & Zach Obront

You're ready to write your book. You've accumulated hard-won knowledge and mastered the solution to a difficult problem. Now you want to put it out into the world— and be recognized for your expertise, like those you've watched reap the benefits of a published book.

You know you have to write it. You've heard it from people for years: you should really write a book. They're right. It's time for you to write the book that cements your legacy and impacts other people—and maybe even the world.

So why haven't you done it yet?

The truth is, writing a book is scary. Is your idea good enough? How do you structure it, write it, and stay motivated? What if you actually finish it, and it's bad? Worst of all: what if you publish it, and no one cares?

If this sounds familiar, The Scribe Method will help you navigate these fears on your journey to becoming a published author. Guided by experts Tucker Max and Zach Obront, you'll overcome the obstacles that have held you back with a simple, time-saving, effective method to writing a great book, and learn the step-by-step process that has created hundreds of bestselling titles.

3) *Lifelong Writing Habit: The Secret to Writing Every Day: Write Faster, Write Smarter*

by Chris Fox

Are you tired of writing intermittently? Would you like to install a lifelong writing habit, one that gets your butt in the chair every single day? Then this is the book for you. Lifelong Writing Habit draws on well tested neuroscience to help you install a daily writing habit that will endure for life.

It contains a simple to understand system, with actionable steps at the end of every chapter. You'll learn:

- How to install a permanent writing habit
- How to get organized
- How to set and achieve writing goals
- How to harness discipline and motivation

It's time to make a permanent shift in your writing. Let's get moving!

4) *The Workplace Writer's Process: A Guide to Getting the Job Done*
by Anne Janzer

If writing is any part of your job, you owe it to yourself to figure out how to get it done consistently, efficiently, and successfully.

This book covers the business communication skills no one teaches you in writing class:

How to streamline collaboration with stakeholders or subject matter experts
Why the style guide is your friend, and how to create one for your business
The most efficient way to approach revision
How to set up your projects to sail through reviews and approvals

The Workplace Writer's Process is filled wth actionable advice that you can use immediately to finish more projects in less time and create content. Buy it today to invest in your career success.

The Workplace Writer's Process won a 2018 IndieReader Discovery Award (2nd place overall in nonfiction) and is a finalist in the 2018 TopShelf Indie Book Awards.

5) *Become a Writer Today*
by Bryan Collins

Do you want to get paid to write?

Or perhaps you want to self-publish a book or become a successful author?

Taking your writing seriously and becoming an author is scary unless you have a little help.

Now, in this MASSIVE series, get three books that will help you with all types of writing" for one low price.

>>>Yes, You Can Write! (Book 1)
Many new writers complain about writer's block. It's time to say goodbye to that problem.

In this practical book, I've gathered 101 of the best writing prompts just for you. Use them for journal writing, fiction, blogging, fiction and even your next book.

The simple truth is you can write almost anything" with a little prompt.

>>>The Savvy Writer's Guide to Productivity (Book 2)
Are you a slow writer?

Discover proven productivity strategies top writers and authors use to succeed. Use them to get the words out and finish writing your stories or book faster.

>>>The Art of Writing a Non-Fiction Book (Book 3)

Who says you can't get paid to write? Almost everybody has an idea for a book, but only a few turn their ideas into a profitable reality.

Now, I explain what need to know about writing, publishing and selling a best-selling non-fiction book, step-by-step.

6) *The Writer's Process: Getting Your Brain in Gear*

by Anne Janzer

Want to be a better writer? Improve your process.

Do you fear the blank page? You may be skipping the essential early phases of writing.

Do you generate swarms of ideas but never publish anything? You need strategies to focus and persist to the finish.

When you learn to work with your brain instead of against it, you'll get more done and have more fun.

Master the Inner Game of Writing

The Writer's Process combines proven practices of successful authors with cognitive science research about how our minds work.

You'll learn:

- How to invite creativity and flow into your writing process
- Why separating writing into different steps makes you more productive

- How to overcome writer's block, negative feedback, and distractions
- How to make time for writing in a busy, interrupt-driven life

Buy it now and find out why so many reviewers say that they wish they'd read it earlier!

The Writer's Process is a 2017 Readers' Favorite Gold Medal award winner and a Foreword INDIES Book of the Year Silver Medal winner.

7) *Stop Worrying; Start Writing: How to Overcome Fear, Self-Doubt and Procrastination*

by Sarah Painter

Do you want to write but can't seem to get started? Are you struggling to finish your novel or frustrated by your slow progress? Perhaps you are starting to worry that you aren't cut out for the writing life…

Let bestselling novelist and host of the Worried Writer podcast, Sarah Painter, show you how to skip past negativity, free-up writing time, cope with self-doubt, and beat procrastination.

Along with mega successful authors such as C.L.Taylor, Mark Edwards, and Julie Cohen, Sarah will show you how to:

- Smash writing blocks to finish stories faster
- Manage self-doubt so that it doesn't stop you creating
- Trick yourself into being more productive
- Schedule your time to maximise your writing output and satisfaction

Plus many more tips and tricks!

Packed with honest, supportive, and hard-won advice, this is your practical guide to getting the work done.

Don't let creative anxiety kill your writing dreams: Stop Worrying and Start Writing today!

'Inspiring, comforting, warm and wise. Both new writers and established authors will find something helpful here.'
Keris Stainton, YA author.

'If Stephen King is your writing godfather then Sarah Painter is the writer's best friend - kind, honest and full of wisdom.' Annie Lyons, bestselling author of The Choir on Hope Street and Not Quite Perfect

'The best book on writing and productivity I have read in a long time. It tackles the fear and self-doubt we all feel when it comes to our writing in such an engagingly honest way, that there are times when I was laughing aloud because here was someone who truly understood. Written with such heart, Sarah, in her characteristically kind, and gentle way that listeners of The Worried Writer podcast have come to love and appreciate, offers solid, actionable advice that will inspire you to approach your writing with enthusiasm and renewed determination!' Lily Graham, author of The Cornish Escape

8) *Declutter Your Mind: How to Stop Worrying, Relieve Anxiety, and Eliminate Negative Thinking*

by S.J. Scott & Barrie Davenport

Feel overwhelmed by your thoughts? Struggling with anxiety about your daily tasks? Or do you want to stop worrying about life?

The truth is...We all experience the occasional negative thought. But if you always feel overwhelmed, then you need to closely examine how these thoughts are negatively impacting your lifestyle.

The solution is to practice specific mindfulness techniques that create more "space" in your mind to enjoy inner peace and happiness. With these habits, you'll have the clarity to prioritize what's most important in your life, what no longer serves your goals, and how you want to live on a daily basis. And that's what you'll learn in Declutter Your Mind.

DOWNLOAD:: Declutter Your Mind -- How to Stop Worrying, Relieve Anxiety, and Eliminate Negative Thinking

The goal of this book is simple: We will teach you the habits, actions, and mindsets to clean up the mental clutter that's holding you back from living a meaningful life.

You will learn:
4 Causes of Mental Clutter

How to Reframe ALL Your Negative Thoughts

4 Strategies to Improve (or Eliminate) Bad Relationships

The Importance of Decluttering the Distractions That Cause Anxiety

A Simple Strategy to Discover What's Important to YOU

400 Words That Help Identify YOUR Values

The Benefit of Meditation and Focused Deep Breathing (and How to Do Both)

How to Create Goals That Connect to Your Passions

Declutter Your Mind is full of exercises that will have an immediate, positive impact on your mindset. Instead of just telling you to do something, we provide practical, science-backed actions that can create real and lasting change if practiced regularly.

9) *Activate Your Brain: How Understanding Your Brain Can Improve Your Work - and Your Life*

by Scott G. Halford

A Wall Street Journal bestseller!
Axiom Business Book Bronze Award Winner

Push your brain to full power, for success at the office and at home

Would you like more control over your life and your work?

Would you like greater stamina as you carry out your daily tasks?

How about more significance and meaning as you move forward in your career?

Scott Halford shows us how we can all find these things if we simply understand how to activate the full potential of the brain. This incredible organ is still full of mystery, but we know enough to harness its power better than ever before. We just have to recognize how the brain works, and understand the actions we can take to help it perform at its best.

Combining research, anecdote, and inspiration, Activate Your Brain shows you how small steps toward better brain function and management can eventually lead to success on a whole new level.

Each chapter offers "Activations"—exercises that help optimize your brain function to . . .
•increase your focus,
•build self-confidence and willpower,
•manage distractions,
•reduce negative stress,
•collaborate effectively with others,
•and much more.

In the end, Activate Your Brain is an indispensable collection of practical things you need to know about your wonderful brain—which, when fully harnessed, can give you more of the fulfilled life you seek.

10) Six Figure Blogging Blueprint: How to Start an Amazingly Profitable Blog in the Next 60 Days (Even If You Have No Experience)

by Raza Imam

Discover how to start an AMAZINGLY profitable blog in the next 60 days (even if you have no experience)

Are you looking for a proven, step-by-step system that allows you to create a profit pulling blog on autopilot - with very little experience?

Are you ready to start making income blogging, but don't know where to begin?

Well, just imagine what it would be like if you easily saw money rolling into your bank account.

Because once you master this process, you'll be able to work from anywhere in the world.

You'll be able to quit your job for good.

And you'll be able to build passive income business profits over the long-term.

In this short but powerful book, I reveal my story of building a passive income blogging business.

You'll discover how to do it, step-by-step.

I'll show you how to get the same results as other ultra-successful bloggers.

Even if you have a full-time job.

In this book, you'll discover:

The BEST Topics to Write About (the SECRET to a wildly successful blog)
Getting Setup the Easy Way (step-by-step) - Hosting, Domain Names, and Content Management System
The Secrets of Designing a Beautiful, Responsive Blog (quickly and easily)
The #1 Secret to Instantly Building Rapport w/ Your Audience
The MIND-BLOWING Content Strategy to Attract Hordes of Eager Readers
How to Create FACE-MELTINGLY Good Blog Posts (they'll go viral and generate massive traffic)
The Step-by-Step to Get Featured on the Biggest Blogs, Podcasts, and Websites in Your Industry (and send a stampede of visitors to your blog)
Email Marketing Magic

And much, much more

It's time to stop gambling with your hard-earned money.

Join the thousands of smart professionals that are leveraging their expertise to make consistent passive income and make money from home from their blog.

I'm an Amazon best-selling author will show you exactly how I broke through fear, frustration, and self-doubt to make a consistent, passive income over the past 2 years (over $25,000)

I reveal the secrets I used to profitably grow my income and watch the money and sales roll into my bank account - like clockwork.

This strategy is powerful, and yet so simple to use.

Even if you are a complete beginner, this strategy will have you earning income streams from your blog in no time.

And if you ever get stuck, you can always reach out to me.

So get started today.

11) Blogging: Getting To $2,000 A Month In 90 Days

by Isaac Kronenberg

Isaac Kronenberg does it again with another fabulous blogging book that goes above and beyond anything else out there!

This latest book by Kronenberg is the most advanced blogging book on the market, teaching nothing but the most effective blogging monetization strategies that exist to get your blog from zero to $2,000 a month in 90 days.

Everything in this book is based on real strategies currently used by top-earning bloggers. Whether you're new to blogging or an advanced blogger, if there was some magic pill that could take you from nothing to earning a full-time income from a blog, then this book is the closest thing in existence to that magic pill.

If you're serious about earning an income blogging, then this book will be the best book which you've ever read on the subject.

12) Ten Quick Wins for Writers: How to ignite creativity, write steadily, and publish your book!

by Jed Jurchenko

Ignite your creativity, grow your writing habit, and write with ease! This writing motivation book is packed with powerful author tools and will guide you on the journey.

Author Tools that Work

Although many people long to publish, only a few achieve this goal. Common writing barriers include:

Writer's block
Fear of failure
Fear of rejection
Inconsistent writing habits
Confusion about what to do next
Worries that publishing will be difficult
Fortunately, you don't have to stay stuck.
These ten author tools will help you write steadily and build up series quick writing wins. In this writing motivation book, you'll discover:

The secret to finishing your book

Two words that change everything
A secret for writing better, fast
How to want to write
Three words that grow persistence
How to beat writer's block
A powerful motivation metaphor
A simple phrase for laser focus
And much more!
First Time Author Help

For years, I wanted to write a book. Unfortunately, I fell into the typical pattern of starting strong, getting sidetracked, and quitting. Then, I discovered the powerful author tools in this book. Today, I write and publish with consistency and have a blast in the process.

Ten Quick Wins for Writers, is packed with first-time author help and creative author tools for established writers. You will discover a multitude of writing strategies founded on time-tested principles. Learn them quickly, develop your writing habit, and become a part of the elite few who publish with consistency. This book is perfect for authors who want to write more, writers searching for new author tools, and everyone who longs to write a book.

Author Help Books

Don't just dream about writing. Use these author tools to grow your writing habit, write steadily, and reach your goals. Ten Quick Wins for Writers, is

part of a series of author help books that also includes
Ten Great Ideas for Authors.

13) *Self-Discipline for Writers: Writing Is Hard, But You Too Can Write and Publish Books Regularly*

by Martin Meadows

You Too Can Become a Successful Writer—If You're Willing to Develop This Trait

Do you know that it's almost impossible to find a successful writer who has published only one book? Virtually every widely acclaimed author has an extensive catalog of books. To join the elite ranks of those who write consistently, you need to learn how to stay prolific over the long term. And for that, the number one ingredient is self-discipline.

In Self-Discipline for Writers, bestselling author Martin Meadows shares his philosophy and strategies on how to build self-discipline as a writer and how to kccp writing over the long term. Here are some of the most important ideas you'll discover:

- 3 foundations of self-discipline for writers (avoid a common mistake that almost always leads to failure),

- 3 steps to a strong work ethic as a writer (learn how to develop a strategy for consistently hitting your word counts),

- 5 types of self-doubt common among writers and how to overcome them (if you don't believe in yourself as a writer, how are your readers supposed to believe in you?),

- 7 tips on how to manage your energy as a writer—including not only the most fundamental advice, but also intricacies like discussing your projects with other people, capturing fleeting ideas, and reading your reviews (learn why optimizing your energy is key to consistent results),

- why control is essential for any writer (and how to claim it),

- 5 good business practices for more self-discipline (this includes some surprising thoughts on how to run your writing business to reduce frustration and increase productivity).

Writing doesn't have to be burdensome. You too can write with more ease, and most importantly, write and publish consistently so that you can enjoy a flourishing writing career. Let's learn together how to accomplish this exciting goal.

14) Make a Living With Blog Writing: How to Write Blog Posts That Clients Pay for and Where to Find Clients - a Beginner's Guide

by Joy Collado

You can get paid to write. This book will show you how.

Five years ago, I started a side hustle: blogging for other people.

As it turns out, making a living writing isn't that hard as long as you know what you're doing.

And this book will show you exactly that – how to earn money blogging for businesses.

Businesses need blogs to drive traffic, stay relevant, and to generate more revenue. That's where you come in is a problogger.

In this book you'll learn everything you need to know from writing blog posts that clients pay for, how to create a blogging portfolio, and build authority in your niche.

This book will also show you how to avoid clients from hell and teach you how to find great clients that not only respect you but also happily pay your rates.

Whether you're a clueless beginner or an experienced pro who's looking to learn more about making a living writing blogs, this book has plenty to offer you.

This book is a step by step guide on how to:
-Lay the groundwork so your freelance business is set up the right way
-Set your blogging goals that will propel you to your success
-Write blog posts that clients pay for
-Find clients that will pay your rates
-Build a blogging portfolio that will impress clients

If you've been wondering how you can make money writing blogs, this book is for you.

And yes, you can work from home. Pants are optional.

Here's what inside:

Part 1 – Getting Started
Make Money Blogging
Your Blogging Goals and Why They Matter

Part 2 – How to Write Blog Posts That Clients Pay For

Your Client's Ideal Reader

Adapting to Your Client's Blogging Voice

Generating Blog Post Ideas

Writing Headlines that Stick

Writing an Enticing Introduction

Writing a Body that Mesmerizes Readers

Writing Inspiring Conclusion

Making Your Writing Shine

Part 3 – How to Find Clients

Finding Your First Paying Clients

Figuring Out How to Price Your Services

Setting Up Your Website

All About Cold Emails

The Power of Guest Posting

Your 30-Day Roadmap to Freelance Blogging Success

Growing Your Freelance Business

Would you like to know more? Grab a copy now and discover how you can make a living doing what you love.

15) *Time Management for Writers: How to write faster, find the time to write your book, and be a more prolific writer*

by Sandra Gerth

In the digital age, publishing as book is easier than ever, but finding the time to write a book is becoming harder and harder. With day jobs, family obligations, household chores, and hobbies, many writers struggle to get any writing done.

At the same time, publishers and readers expect writers to publish multiple books every year and to somehow find enough time to market their books through blogging, social media, and networking.

If you are struggling to find enough time to write or don't get much written once you finally do, this book is for you.

16) *The Prosperity Bible: The Greatest Writings of All Time on the Secrets to Wealth and Prosperity*

by Wallace D. Wattles

In a beautiful, durable volume suited to a lifetime of use, here is the all-in-one "bible" on how to harness the creative powers of your mind to achieve a life of prosperity-packaged in a handsome display box with a ribbon bookmark.

The Prosperity Bible is a one-of-a-kind resource that collects the greatest moneymaking secrets of authors from every field-religion, finance, philosophy, and self-help-and makes them available in an attractive, keepsake edition. This is a book to treasure and return to again and again for guidance, ideas, know-how, and inspiration.

Here is the only single volume where you can read success advice from Napoleon Hill, P. T. Barnum, Benjamin Franklin, Charles Fillmore, Wallace D. Wattles, Florence Scovel Shinn, and Ernest Holmes-along with a bevy of million-copy-selling writers who have one key element in common: a commitment to understanding and promulgating the laws of winning.

These are the beloved teachers and writers who created the idea of a mental formula for success. Their principles, comprehensively collected in nineteen selected writings, have been proved in the experience of millions of men and women who have cherished their works from the late nineteenth century to the present day. Now they are enshrined in this all-in-one treasury-complete in a handsome display box with a ribbon bookmark.

17) Writing Successful Self-Help and How-To Books (WILEY BOOKS FOR WRITERS SERIES)

by Jean Marie Stine

"If you follow only a third of Jean's advice, you'll have a successful book." --Jeremy Tarcher, Publisher Jeremy P. Tarcher, Inc.

"After Jean reworked my first draft, paperback rights sold for $137,000." --Timmen Cermak, M.D., author of A Time to Heal: The Road to Recovery for Adult Children of Alcoholics

Mastering the craft and understanding the mechanics of writing self-help and how-to books is the key to getting publishers to take notice of your work. Now, in the first guide to writing self-help and how-to books, Jean Stine offers an insider's view of this growing genre. Her easy-to-follow program takes you step-by-step through the complete writing process. You'll learn the importance of:
* Structure and Style
* Clear, easy-to-understand exercises
* Creating catchy and compelling titles, subtitles, and chapter headings
* Using lists, charts, and graphs to maximum effect

* Checklists and other interactive elements
* Writing a proposal that sells
* Negotiating permissions for quotations, photos, and illustrations
* Preparing your manuscript for presentation to a publisher

18) *A Professor's Guide to Writing Essays: The No-Nonsense Plan for Better Writing*

by Jacob Neumann

This isn't a typical book on writing essays. First, it's for college students, graduate students, and even high school students - good writing is good writing; all that changes is the length and complexity of what you write. But the plan stays the same. Second, I'm not going to tell you any cute stories about writing. I'm not going to tell you the standard information about writing. Nor am I going to give you a simple formula for writing an essay. They don't work, and in the long run, they won't help you. What I am going to do is give you a plan for how you should approach writing essays.

This plan works. If you follow it and practice it, you will learn to write much better essays - all types of essays. Because all essays are essentially the same. Most teachers and books will tell you differently. But I think they are wrong. The rules for good writing don't change depending on a certain "type" of essay. The only thing that changes is how you make your case, how you make your argument (and we cover that in Step 5). In this plan, we're not going to cover every aspect of academic writing.

We're going to focus on the things that you absolutely have to do in order to create good essays.

How do I know all of this? I've been teaching since 1996. I've taught at every level of schooling, and I've taught students from around the world. Now I work as an associate professor at The University of Texas Rio Grande Valley where I teach people how to teach. I also publish my own academic writing in some of the top journals in my field (you can look up my work on Google Scholar). So, not only do I know what students need to learn to create great essays, I put this information to the test in my own academic work. And in this book, I boil down all of my experience teaching writing plus my experience as a scholar into a simple, direct, and efficient plan that will improve the quality of your essays.

19) How To Write Non-Fiction: Turn Your Knowledge Into Words

by Joanna Penn

Do you want to write a non-fiction book but don't know where to start? Or perhaps you worry that you're not 'the expert' or have enough authority in your niche to write a book on it?

Are you ready to help other people and change your own life with your words?

The first non-fiction book I wrote changed my life. Sure, it helped other people, but mostly it altered the course of my life – so much so that 10 years later, I make a living with my writing.

I've written seven other non-fiction books and co-written two more and built a multi-six-figure income around my non-fiction eco-system. In this book, I'll share everything I've learned along the way and save you time, effort and frustration on your author journey.

The book includes:

PART 1. Before You Write: Mindset

Why write a non-fiction book?

Author-centered marketing. The power of a personal brand

Build your author website

Build an email list

Integrate email marketing with your book

Content marketing for non-fiction books

My non-fiction marketing journey

Conclusion and your next steps.

It's time to (finally) write your non-fiction book.

20) *Unlimited Memory: How to Use Advanced Learning Strategies to Learn Faster, Remember More and be More Productive*

by Kevin Horsley

Kevin Horsley Broke a World Memory Record in 2013...

And You're About to Learn How to Use His Memory Strategies to Learn Faster, Be More Productive and Achieve More Success

With over 200,000 copies sold, Unlimited Memory is a Wall Street Journal Best Seller and has been the #1 memory book on Amazon for more than two years. It has been translated into more than a dozen languages including French, Chinese, Russian, Korean, Ukrainian, and Lithuanian.

Most people never tap into 10% of their potential for memory.

In this book, you're about to learn:

How the World's Top Memory Experts Concentrate and Remember Any Information at Will, and How You Can Too

Do you ever feel like you're too busy, too stressed or just too distracted to concentrate and get work done?

In Unlimited Memory, you'll learn how the world's best memory masters get themselves to concentrate at will, anytime they want. When you can easily focus and concentrate on the task at hand, and store and recall useful information, you can easily double your productivity and eliminate wasted time, stress and mistakes at work.

In this book, you'll find all the tools, strategies and techniques you need to improve your memory.

Here's just a taste of the memory methods you'll learn in this book:

The 3 bad habits that keep you from easily remembering important information

How a simple pattern of thinking can stop you from imprinting and remembering key facts, figures and ideas, and how to break this old pattern so you'll never again be known as someone with a "bad memory"

How to master your attention so you can focus and concentrate longer, even during challenging or stressful situations

How to use your car to remember anything you want (like long lists or information you need to remember for your studies or personal life) without writing anything down

Simple methods that allow you to nail down tough information or complex concepts quickly and easily

How to combine your long-term memory (things you already know and will never forget) and short-term memory (information you want to remember right now) to create instant recall for tests, presentations and important projects

The simple, invisible mental technique for remembering names without social awkwardness or anxiety

How using your imagination to bring boring information to life can help you dramatically improve your attention span and recall

An incredible strategy for remembering numbers (the same system Kevin used to remember Pi to 10,000 digits and beat the world memory record by 14 minutes)

How to use a mental map to lock in and connect hundreds or even thousands of ideas in your long-term memory (this method will allow you to become a leading expert in your field faster than you ever dreamed possible)

If you're ready to harness the incredible power of your mind to remember more in less time, this book is for you.

About the Author

For over 25 years, Kevin Horsley has been analyzing the mind and memory and its capacity for brilliance. He is one of only a few people in the world to have received the title of International Grandmaster of Memory. He is a World Memory Championship medalist, and a two-time World Record holder for The Everest of memory tests. Kevin is also an author of four books, and the designer of a mathematics game with the Serious Games Institute at North-West University Vaal Campus.

His work has been featured in The Oprah Magazine, Time, Forbes, Inc., The Huffington Post, ELLE, Longevity and on numerous TV and radio shows.

Kevin is an International professional speaker and has spoken in many different countries. He assists organizations in improving their learning, motivation, creativity and thinking.

Made in the USA
San Bernardino,
CA